Uncharted Horizons

Gauri Gokhale

Presentation by *BookLeaf Publishing*

Web: www.bookleafpub.com

E-mail: info@bookleafpub.com

ISBN:9789360943745

First edition 2024

To the uncharted horizons deep within the core of my mind and heart, where poetry slides on the winds of artistry, hoping these compositions become an orbit leading the readers to the undiscovered empire of their own sentients.

ACKNOWLEDGEMENT

I extend my gratitude to those who have escorted this symbolic voyage with me, cuddling the stanzas of my inspiration. Your assistance is the melody that harmonizes with the words penned down by me. My sincere appreciation for being part of this poetic association.

PREFACE

Uncharted horizons spills the chords that linger between the lines.

In the calm corners of reflections, these poems took birth. Connect with me in this beginning.

Welcome to the prelude of my poetic adventures.

Table of Contents

Childhood Innocence

In the cradle of dawn's tender light,
Where innocence bathes in pure delight,
Childhood dances with carefree glee,
In the embrace of timeless reverie.
Beneath the canopy of azure skies,
Where laughter's melody softly flies,
In fields adorned with flowers fair,
Innocence wanders without a care.
Through meadows kissed by the sun's
warm rays,
Innocence weaves its golden days,
With eyes aglow and hearts so pure,
Childhood's innocence shall endure.
In the secret realms of make-believe,
Where dreams and fantasies interweave,

Innocence reigns, a sovereign grace,
A sanctuary in life's bustling race.
In whispered secrets and playful games,
Innocence thrives, untouched by shames,
With hands that reach for stars above,
In childhood's innocence, we find love.
In every giggle, in every tear,
Innocence whispers, "Have no fear,"
For in its arms, we find solace sweet,
In childhood's innocence, hearts meet.
Oh, cherish this treasure, so pure and
bright,
Hold onto innocence with all your might,
For in its embrace, we find our truth,
In childhood's innocence, eternal youth.

Memories

Through the vault of time, where memories
reside,
A medley woven, with threads of life's tide,
Each moment a pearl, in the ocean of mind,
Each memory a story, unique and refined.
In the corridors of remembrance, we roam,
Exploring the echoes of moments long
known,
From the laughter that danced in the
summer air,
To the whispers of love, tender and rare.
Memories are like chapters, penned in our
souls,
Each page a journey, each memory unfolds,

Through the tapestry of joys and sorrows,
We find the essence of our tomorrows.
In the soft glow of nostalgia's light,
We revisit the past, in the still of night,
We relive the joys, we confront the pain,
We dance with ghosts in memory's domain.
From the innocence of childhood's
embrace,
To the trials of youth, the challenges we
face,
Each memory a beacon, guiding our way,
Through the labyrinth of night and day.
Memories are the echoes of time,
The echoes of laughter, the echoes of
rhyme,
They shape who we are, they shape who
we'll be,
They're the whispers of immortality.
So let us cherish each memory dear,
For they're the treasures that we hold near,
In the tapestry of life, they'll forever reside,
A testament to the journey, the waves of the
tide.

Reflections in Water

In the mirror of the water's face,
Reflections dance with gentle grace.
A symphony of light and shade,
In the tranquil depths, they cascade.
Rippling whispers tell a tale,
Of skies above and winds that sail.
Each wave a brushstroke, smooth and fine,
Painting memories, divine.
See the trees lean in to peer,
Their verdant forms so crisp and clear.
Birds take flight in mirrored skies,
Their fleeting shadows mesmerize.
Clouds drift by, their shapes transform,
In liquid glass, they break and swarm.
The sun, a golden orb on high,

Kisses the water with a sigh.
In this watery looking glass,
Time stands still, as moments pass.
We see ourselves, both near and far,
Reflected in the water's star.
So let us gaze and ponder deep,
The secrets that the waters keep.
For in their depths, we may find,
Reflections of our heart and mind.

Mirror

When in a chamber dimly lit, where
shadows dance and flicker,
Stands a solitary mirror, reflecting all it
sees.
Its surface smooth as glass, yet holding
secrets deeper,
A silent witness to the tales of joy and woe.
In its frame of polished oak, it hangs with
quiet grace,
Capturing moments fleeting, etching
memories in its gaze.
Each glance into its depths unveils a
different story,
A symphony of souls, a medley of life.

Behold the mirror's magic, where truth and
beauty blend,
Where flaws become like poetry, and scars
begin to mend.
It whispers ancient wisdom, as if from
distant shores,
A gentle reminder of the journey evermore.
In its silvered surface, we confront our very
selves,
Reflections of our hopes and fears, our
dreams upon the shelves.
It holds the power to reveal, to heal, to
understand,
A portal to the soul, in this enchanted land.
Oh mirror, mirror on the wall, what secrets
do you keep?
What mysteries lie hidden in the shadows,
dark and deep?
You are a silent sentinel, a guardian of
truth,
Reflecting back the essence of the fleeting
days of youth.
So let us gaze into your depths, and ponder
what we see,

For in your silent wisdom, lies the key to
being free.
In your timeless reflection, we find our own
true worth,
A mirror to the soul, a witness to our birth.

One Winter Morning

One winter morning, crisp and clear,
Nature's breath hung in the air, so dear.
A blanket of frost, adorned the ground,
As the sun's golden rays gently found.
The world was painted in hues of white,
Sparkling diamonds in the soft sunlight.
Trees stood silent, clad in icy lace,
A serene landscape, a heavenly embrace.
Birds chirped softly, their songs so sweet,
As they danced amidst the frosty sheet.
Footsteps echoed on the frozen ground,
In the quiet stillness, a tranquil sound.
With each breath, a misty sigh,
Underneath the vast, azure sky.

Nature slumbered, in peaceful repose,
On this winter morning, where time froze.
In the distance, a river flowed,
Its waters whispering secrets untold.
Majestic mountains stood tall and proud,
Their peaks adorned with snowy shroud.
One winter morning, a fleeting dream,
Where the world sparkled and gleamed.
A moment frozen in time's embrace,
Etched in memory's sacred space.

Forgotten Self

Amidst the depths of cuddling memories,
where shadows dwell,
Lies the forgotten self, a tale untold, a silent
knell.
Lost betwixt the labyrinth of time's
relentless flow,
It lingers in the corners of the mind, a
whisper low.
Once vibrant and alive, with dreams as vast
as the sky,
Now buried beneath layers of life's hurried
sigh.

A specter of the past, a ghost of what once
was,
The forgotten self yearns to break free, to
once again buzz.
In the rush of days and the chaos of nights,
It fades into obscurity, robbed of its rights.
But deep within the recesses of the soul's
domain,
It waits patiently for the chance to rise
again.
For even in the darkest hour, there lies a
spark,
A glimmer of hope, lighting up the dark.
And as the weary heart seeks solace in the
night,
The forgotten self stirs, ready to take flight.
With each breath drawn, it begins to
remember,
The echoes of laughter, the embers of
ember.
It reclaims its essence, piece by precious
piece,
Until at last, it finds its long-awaited
release.

No longer shackled by the chains of doubt
and fear,
The forgotten self emerges, crystal clear.
With newfound strength and purpose, it
takes its place,
In the grand tapestry of life with grace.
So let us not forget the selves we left
behind,
For they hold the keys to treasures
undefined.
Embrace them tenderly, with love and care,
For in their resurrection, we find the truth
we seek to share.

The Moonlit Night

Amidst the hush of night, beneath the
moon's soft glow,
Where shadows dance in a rhythmic flow,
The world transforms in silvery light,
As dreams take flight on wings of night.
The moon, a beacon in the velvet sky,
Casting its spell, enchanting the eye,
Its gentle radiance, a soothing balm,
In the stillness of the moonlit calm.
Beneath the canopy of stars above,
The earth is bathed in a moonlit love,
Each whisper of wind, each rustle of tree,
Carries the magic of night's decree.
In the moonlit night, secrets unfold,

As mysteries deepen, tales untold,
The nightingale sings its sweet refrain,
In harmony with the lunar domain.
The world is bathed in a silver sheen,
A tranquil oasis, serene and serene,
In the moonlit night, we find solace deep,
As the world around us gently sleeps.
So let us wander in the moon's embrace,
And lose ourselves in its tender grace,
For in the moonlit night, we find our way,
Guided by its ethereal display.

A Pallet of Colours

Upon the canvas of the sky,
A palette of colors begins to fly.
Brush strokes of dawn in shades so bright,
Painting the world with morning light.
Golden hues kiss the horizon's rim,
As the day awakens, the world begins.
Amber and rose blend in harmony,
Creating a masterpiece for all to see.
As noon approaches, the colors shift,
Azure skies above, a vibrant gift.
Fields of green and flowers bold,
Nature's tapestry, a sight to behold.
The sun descends with a fiery kiss,

Casting shadows long, a twilight bliss.
Oranges and purples dance in the air,
As twilight whispers, "night's drawing
near."
Under the cloak of darkness deep,
Stars emerge from their celestial keep.
Silver and indigo paint the night,
A symphony of colors, pure and bright.
In every corner, in every hue,
A story waiting to break through.
For life is but a canvas, vast and grand,
Filled with colors by nature's hand.
So let us revel in the palette's array,
In the beauty of colors that never sway.
For in each shade, in every hue,
We find the magic of life anew.

Deep Blue Ocean

Beneath the vast expanse of sky's grace,
Lies a world of wonder, a boundless space,
Where waves dance with the rhythm of the
moon,
And secrets lurk in the deep blue ocean's
tune.
In the heart of the ocean, where depths
unknown,
Lie treasures untold, in a watery throne,
A kingdom of creatures, both fierce and
fair,
In the deep blue ocean, life's mysteries
dare.
The waves, like whispers, lull the soul to
sleep,
As the ocean's embrace is vast and deep,
Its depths hold stories of ages past,

In the silent depths, memories last.
From the coral reefs to the sandy floor,
The ocean's beauty we cannot ignore,
With hues of blue, from dark to light,
In the deep blue ocean, dreams take flight.
Beneath the surface, where silence reigns,
Life thrives in the ocean's domains,
From the smallest krill to the mighty whale,
In the deep blue ocean, life sets sail.
Yet beneath its beauty lies a hidden might,
For the ocean commands both fear and
fright,
With storms that rage and waves that roar,
The deep blue ocean demands respect and
more.
But amidst its power, there's a sense of
calm,
A tranquil oasis, a soothing balm,
For in the deep blue ocean, there's a peace,
Where worries fade and troubles cease.
So let us marvel at the ocean's grace,
And cherish the wonders in its embrace,
For in the deep blue ocean, we find our
place,
In the vast expanse of time and space.

Secrets of the heart

In the chamber of the soul, where shadows
softly play,
Lie the secrets of the heart, hidden from
the light of day.
A labyrinth of whispers, woven in the dark,
Each echo a reminder of the journey, deep
and stark.
Within this sacred sanctuary, emotions rise
and fall,
Like waves upon the ocean, they heed their
silent call.
Love, a tender blossom, blooming in the
night,
Its petals fragile, yet its roots dig deep,
holding tight.

Yet amidst the blooms, there lie thorns
unseen,
The wounds of past betrayals, where trust
has ever been.
Fear, a specter haunting, lurking in the
gloom,
Binding hearts in chains of doubt, casting
shadows of doom.
Hope, a flickering candle, burning against
the night,
Guiding weary souls through the darkness,
towards the light.
Faith, a steady anchor, amidst the stormy
sea,
An unwavering belief in love's enduring
legacy.
But deeper still, beyond the surface of the
soul,
Lie the dreams and desires that make us
truly whole.
Yearnings unspoken, buried deep within,
Longing for connection, for a love that's
pure and kin.
For the secrets of the heart are vast and
wide,

A tapestry of longing, woven side by side.
Each thread a memory, each stitch a silent
plea,
To find the one who holds the key to set our
spirits free.
So let us honor these secrets, held within
our breast,
For they are the essence of what makes us
truly blessed.
In the chambers of the heart, where
shadows softly play,
Lie the secrets of our souls, guiding us
along the way.

The Art of Rain

While the night is still, when all is calm,
The heavens open up, releasing their balm.
A symphony begins, a gentle refrain,
As nature dances to the art of rain.
Each droplet falls with grace, a silent
prayer,
Quenching the earth, with love and care.
The scent of petrichor fills the air,
A fragrant reminder that life is fair.
The leaves on trees, they shimmer and
sway,
As raindrops kiss them in a tender display.
The world is washed anew, in shades of
gray,
And for a moment, all worries fade away.
Rivers swell and streams come alive,

As raindrops descend from the skies above.
They carve their path, with relentless drive,
A testament to nature's boundless love.
In every drop, a story is told,
Of journeys taken and dreams untold.
Of parched lands quenched and hearts
consoled,
In the art of rain, mysteries unfold.
So let us revel in this wondrous sight,
As raindrops fall in the still of night.
For in their dance, there is pure delight,
In the art of rain, everything is right.

Butterfly's Flight

In the meadow, bathed in golden light,
A butterfly takes its wondrous flight.
With wings of silk, adorned in hues,
It dances gracefully, as if to amuse.
Born from the cocoon, a metamorphosis
rare,
From caterpillar to beauty, beyond
compare.
It flutters and flits, in the gentle breeze,
A symbol of transformation, of life's
mysteries.
Through fields of flowers, it gracefully
glides,
Savoring the sweetness that nature
provides.

Each delicate flutter, a stroke of art,
Painting the sky with its vibrant heart.
It whispers secrets to the petals below,
Of journeys taken, of places to go.
Its fragile wings, a symbol of grace,
Navigating the winds, finding its place.
Oh, butterfly, with your beauty so bright,
You fill the world with sheer delight.
A reminder of life's transient dance,
Of second chances, of new romance.
So let us follow the butterfly's flight,
Embrace the change, embrace the light.
For like the butterfly, we too can soar,
And discover the wonders life has in store.

Threads of Destiny

In the blends of fate, where destinies
entwine,
Threads of life are woven, a story so divine.
Each strand a journey, unfolding with each
breath,
Weaving tales of triumph, and trials met
with strength.
From the first stitch cast upon life's sacred
loom,
To the final knot tied in the fabric's womb,
The threads of destiny intertwine and
weave,

Guiding us through paths both humble and
naive.
Some threads are spun with golden gleam,
Filled with joy, like a hopeful dream.
Others are dark, with shadows deep,
Where tears are shed, and sorrows keep.
Yet in the weaving of this cosmic design,
Each thread serves purpose, each line
defines,
The intricate dance of life's grand scheme,
Where every twist and turn is but a gleam.
For in the threads of destiny, we find,
A tapestry rich, with patterns entwined.
Each life a stitch in the grand design,
Bound by fate's eternal twine.
So let us cherish each thread we hold dear,
Embrace the journey, without fear.
For in the tapestry of destiny's flow,
We find the beauty in letting go.

Dancing Shadows

In the twilight's gentle embrace they play,
Those elusive dancers, in shades of gray,
As day bids farewell and night draws near,
The world transforms, and shadows
appear.
With graceful movements, they twirl and
spin,
Like ethereal beings, they dance within,
A silent ballet, a mesmerizing sight,
In the fading glow of the dying light.
They stretch and sway with every breeze,
Their movements fluid, their forms at ease,
In the dance of shadows, time suspends,

As darkness and light blend and blend.
They mimic the trees, the leaves, the
flowers,
Their shapes ever-changing, like fleeting
hours,
They paint the earth with their silent art,
A symphony of shadows, close to the heart.
In the glow of the moon, they come alive,
Their dance transcending, they strive to
thrive,
They whisper secrets in the still of night,
In the language of shadows, pure and
bright.
They dance on walls, on ceilings, on floors,
Their presence felt behind closed doors,
In every corner, in every nook,
The dancing shadows write their book.
They mirror our movements, our hopes,
our fears,
They reflect our joys, our trials, our tears,
In the dance of shadows, we find our kin,
For they are a part of us, deep within.
So let us embrace them, these dancing
shades,
And marvel at the beauty that never fades,

For in their dance, we find our own,
In the rhythm of shadows, we are home.

Mysteries of the Universe

In the vast expanse of cosmic night,
Where stars ignite with radiant light,
Lies the realm of mysteries untold,
Where secrets of the universe unfold.
Through galaxies, vast and grand,
We journey far across the land,
Exploring realms beyond our sight,
In the endless depths of cosmic flight.
From swirling nebulas, where stars are
born,
To black holes, where light is torn,
We ponder questions, profound and deep,
As we traverse the heavens, in silence, we
creep.
What forces shape the cosmic dance,

Guiding stars in their celestial trance?
What unseen hands, what cosmic power,
Weaves the fabric of space, hour by hour?
In the whispers of the cosmic wind,
We seek the answers, where they're pinned,
But the universe remains a mystery,
A puzzle vast, shrouded in history.
Yet in the mystery, there lies beauty,
In the unknown, there's a sense of duty,
To explore, to wonder, to dream and dare,
To reach beyond the limits, to places rare.
So let us gaze upon the cosmic sea,
And embrace the mysteries, wild and free,
For in the vastness of the universe's
expanse,
We find the wonders of life's eternal dance.

Dreams and Aspirations

These silent chambers of the night's
embrace,
Where stars ignite the sky with grace,
There, in the depths of slumber's realm,
Dreams unfurl, like a sacred helm.
With eyes closed tight, the mind takes
flight,
To realms unseen, in the cloak of night,
Dreams, like whispers from distant shores,
Call to us, unlocking hidden doors.
In dreams, we soar on wings of hope,
Across horizons where possibilities elope,
We chase the stars, we touch the moon,
In the canvas of dreams, we find our tune.
Through valleys deep and mountains high,

In dreams, our aspirations touch the sky,
We dare to reach, we dare to strive,
For in the pursuit of dreams, we feel alive.
In the tapestry of dreams, we paint our
fate,
With colors bold, we navigate,
The winding paths, the unknown lands,
With dreams as our compass, we take a
stand.
For dreams are the whispers of the soul,
The fuel that ignites, the ultimate goal,
They beckon us forth, they light the way,
Guiding us through the night and day.
So let us dream, let us aspire,
To heights unknown, to hearts afire,
For in the pursuit of dreams, we find our
truth,
In the tapestry of life, dreams are our
youth.

Moments of Peace

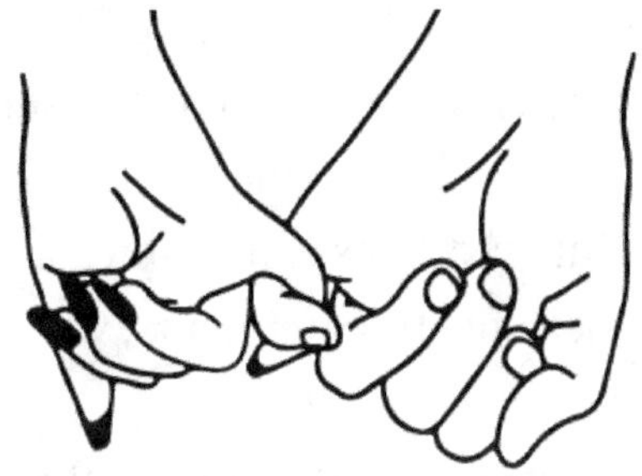

In the stillness of the dawn, before the
world awakes,
Lies a moment of peace, where tranquility
takes.
The sun's first rays gently kiss the earth,
As silence reigns, in this moment of rebirth.
In the embrace of nature, where rivers flow,
And mountains stand tall, covered in snow,
There's a serenity that washes over all,
In the whispering breeze, in the songbird's
call.
In the quiet corners of our own minds,
Where worries fade and peace finds,
There's a sanctuary, a sacred space,
Where we find solace, in this tranquil place.

In the warmth of a loved one's embrace,
Or the laughter shared in a familiar place,
There's a comfort, a sense of ease,
In these moments of peace, we find release.
So let us cherish these moments, small but
profound,
Where inner stillness and calm are found.
For in these fleeting moments, we come to
see,
That peace is not just a state, but a way to
be.

Loss and Grief

In the heart's caverns, where shadows
dwell,
Echoes of loss, like tolling bells,
Grief, a relentless, tidal wave,
Crashing through the soul's dark cave.
Memories flicker, flames now dim,
In the silence, echoes hymn,
Each tear a testament, a sigh,
To love's embrace, now passing by.
In the garden of remembrance, we roam,
Seeking solace, finding home,
But the petals wilt, the colors fade,
As we navigate this somber shade.
Yet amidst the ruins, a whisper of grace,
A glimmer of hope, a gentle embrace,

For though the pain may never subside,
In the brokenness, love still abides.
So we gather the fragments, piece by piece,
In the mosaic of sorrow, we find release,
For in loss, we discover the depth of our
heart,
And in grief, we learn to embrace the art.
For every tear shed, a seed is sown,
In the fertile soil of the unknown,
And from the ashes, new life will rise,
A phoenix reborn beneath grieving skies.
So let us honor the ache, the tender strife,
For in loss and grief, we find life's truest
rife,
And though the road be fraught with
despair,
Love's enduring flame will guide us there.

Healing and Renewal

There is a garden of the soul, where
wounds reside,
Lies the promise of healing, deep inside.
Like tender shoots breaking through the
earth,
Renewal begins with a quiet rebirth.
From the ashes of pain, new strength
arises,
As broken hearts mend and scars surprise
us.
With each breath taken, a step towards
light,
Healing and renewal, a sacred rite.
In the gentle rain that washes away,
The stains of sorrow, the fears that sway.

We find solace in the cleansing stream,
A purifying balm, in healing's dream.
Through the cracks of brokenness, light
seeps in,
Illuminating the path where hope begins.
In the tender embrace of love's warm glow,
We find the courage to let wounds go.
With time as our ally, wounds slowly fade,
As the heart finds peace in the serenade,
Of life's endless song, where renewal flows,
And healing's gentle touch bestows.
So let us embrace the journey of the heart,
With faith as our compass, and love as our
art.
For in the dance of healing and renewal,
We find the essence of life's eternal jewel.

Embracing Change

The quiet whispers of the wind's soft sigh,
Lies the promise of change, as seasons fly.
Cuddling the shifting tides, the ebb and
flow,
For in change's caress, new paths we sow.
Like leaves adrift on autumn's breeze,
We dance with change, amidst the trees.
Colors fade, yet beauty remains,
In the cycle of life, where nothing wanes.
As winter's frost gives way to spring's
embrace,
New life emerges, in nature's grace.
From barren branches, blooms appear,
A reminder that change brings renewal
near.

In the summer sun, we find our stride,
Embracing change, with hearts open wide.
Fields of green stretch to the horizon's
bend,
As we journey forward, around each bend.
Through the highs and lows, the twists and
turns,
We learn and grow, as change discerns.
For in every shift, every rise and fall,
We find the strength to conquer all.
So let us welcome change with open arms,
Embracing its gifts, its endless charms.
For in its embrace, we find our way,
Guided by the promise of a brighter day.

Hope

At the darkest hour, when shadows loom,
And despair grips tight, like a heavy tomb,
There shines a beacon, a guiding light,
A flicker of hope in the endless night.
It whispers softly, amidst the storm's roar,
A promise of better days, worth fighting for.
In the depths of despair, it takes a stand,
A steadfast ally, a helping hand.
Hope is the melody in the silence of grief,
The balm for the wounded, seeking relief.
It is the sunrise after the coldest night,
The promise of dawn, burning ever bright.
With wings unfurled, it soars above,

Filling hearts with courage, strength, and
love.
It knows no boundaries, no limits, no end,
A timeless force, on which we depend.
In the face of adversity, it dares to believe,
That even in darkness, we can achieve.
It is the seed of resilience, planted deep
within,
Nourished by faith, against all odds to win.
So let hope be your compass, your guiding
star,
Leading you onward, no matter how far.
For in its embrace, miracles unfold,
And dreams take flight, no longer on hold.
Though trials may come, and challenges
may abound,
With hope as your ally, you'll stand your
ground.
For in its embrace, you'll find the strength
to cope,
And emerge victorious, fueled by hope.

www.ingramcontent.com/pod-product-compliance
Lightning Source LLC
LaVergne TN
LVHW021251200726
843509LV00012B/1640